# LIGH

## An Inspirational Novel Series 1

# OGECHI OHAEGBU - SHADAMORO

outskirtspress

DENVER, COLORADO

Outskirts Press, Inc.
http://www.outskirtspress.com

ISBN: 978-1-4787-0503-1

Library of Congress Control Number: 2013909032

Outskirts Press and the "OP" logo are trademarks belonging to Outskirts Press, Inc.

PRINTED IN THE UNITED STATES OF AMERICA

# ACKNOWLEGEMENT

This book is dedicated to God Almighty for his great works and what he is about to use me to do for all his beloved children in the whole world. To my Family, especially my children Funsho and Feyi whose smiles always give me joy every day, their abundant love for me is priceless. To my cousins and friends Chinyere, Nkiru, Ugonna, Remi, Ihuoma, Chinelo, Selina, Cathy, Mma, Ijeoma, Uche, Pamela, Clara, Uncle Jude, Aunty Monique, Pascal, Okwy, Ihuoma, Remi, Dr Jerry and Rita, Ramona and Rick, Chris and Jack, Charito and Mark whose words of encouragement at my lowest moments, inspired me to find my passion. To my brothers and sisters and their families-Kelly and Stanley, Obinna and Ekene, Chidimma and Okam, Uzoma and Ijeoma, Uloma and Isidore, Chijioke, and Mezu for always being there for me in my time of need. To the city of Vernon hills, Lake County and St. Mary of Vernon church for their love and support to my family. To my parents Professor Aloysius and Euna Ohaegbu for raising me to be what I am today, thank you. Finally to everyone in this world who is hurting in one way or the other in everyday aspects of life, may this book bring joy and happiness to your lives.

# CONTENTS

**THE LIGHT THAT SHINES BESIDE ME**

# CHAPTER 1

# FINDING HAPPINESS

As I looked out of my window, a bright light came into my room, the fresh breeze was so refreshing, and it was sunny outside; it felt like 68 degrees out there. Thank goodness, it's that time of the year, we are soon approaching summer, the fresh flowers are sprung and the grasses look greener. The birds are flying in the sky. I almost forgot what it felt like to be warm again after a long period of winter and cold weather.

I quickly went down the kitchen, a cold drink is what I need now to cool my nerves. What can be so delightful as a cold glass of orange juice on a warm sunny day! I swept past the laundry room, there were many clothes that needed to be washed, no thanks to my job search, and it took almost the whole day for me, searching and applying for jobs online on my computer. I don't regret staying this long on my computer, in fact, it made me feel better that I was constantly trying to find a job without losing hope in this present economic recession and high rate of unemployment.

The past weeks have been exhausting and mind bugging. Bills are long time overdue and coming in like it never ends. I avoid checking my mailbox daily, my heart pounds to see piles of mails. Loosing my job has been tough on me and my family. It's becoming hard for us to put food on the table for our kids, it's a bad situation, we are almost losing our home. The thought of these problems have kept me so unhappy, I'm losing my mind.

Just as I was about to take a shower, Jordan my 3 months old baby woke up from sleep. He is such a cutey-pie, his smile brightens my day. He looked at me with so much curiosity in his eyes, his lips are moving, and he wants to eat. Nursing Jordan has saved us a lot of money from buying baby milk. Sometimes I think that it's a mystery that, my first son Jason did not nurse full time, he preferred formula which really cost us a lot then, and thank goodness I had a job then. Now I'm unemployed, Jordan prefers to be breast-fed, he has rejected baby formula. Jordan's birth was a special gift to me, he made it so easy for me to adapt to the present economic situation. It did not take long after feeding Jordan; he went right back to sleep again, routine babies in his age love.

Its Lunch time, Jason is hungry, he needs his lunch. I go back to the kitchen; a chicken sandwich is what we need. It was a nice lunch; I did not know how relaxing it can be to have lunch with my kid on the dinner table. Jason is a very loving and caring child; he poured apple juice in a cup for me and said: cheers! At that moment, I forgot my worries and enjoyed my lunch. It only takes one beautiful moment to see that there is more to life than worries. It cost nothing to be happy. Happiness comes in our everyday life. It can be a smile on your kid's face, it can be eating dinner together on the dinner table as a family, it can be a song from a radio, it can be taking a walk and enjoying the fresh breeze, it can be looking at the birds flying, and it can be enjoying the free gift of nature; our surrounding, it can be singing a song that you like in the shower and so on. We just need to observe and find it in our everyday life.

# CHAPTER 2

# THE CALL

Another beautiful day is here, I can't believe its Tuesday already, a lot has to be done yet with the house cleaning. I need to go to grocery shopping; it's all a recurring cycle, what a great way to start my day.

I put on the TV, and connection was lost. I also tried to go to the internet on my computer, but internet was off too. Both TV and internet are connected with the same provider. It just occurred to me, we have not paid the bills yet, and it's probably interrupted. Now what will happen to my job search? How do I know what is going on around me and in the world? How do I keep applying for a job?

A voice came into my mind, it says to me in a soft tone, a tone that is soothing and calming. It says "my dear", why are you so hard on yourself? Why do you stress yourself like this? Why do you have to worry about what will happen to your job search? Your destiny is in your hands, right here beside you. You don't need to stay late at night in the computers, you don't need to look at the TV all day to know what is happening, if you do know what is happening, can you change any of that? Really, the answer was no. We can't change anything that has destined to happen.

Later that day, I then got a call from a childhood friend chinyere. Chinyere is such a wonderful person, with great personality. Anytime she calls me, she has a way of making me laugh and brightens my day with her sense of humor. We grew up in the same community at the University of Nigeria Campus. Our parents were professors in the school and all instructors of the college lived on campus staff buildings. She is like a sister to me. She encouraged me to search for my passion, there must be something that you love to do" she says". It was a couple of months after the Easter holidays. When she hung up, it was as if God has spoken to me through her.

At this point, I remembered my writing; I'm good at expressing my feelings about things around me. I thought loudly; I also would like to give to the needy, and to the poor, but how do I give when we are barely surviving. Aha! I can write Inspirational books to encourage people to live a happy live, to share with one another, to give to the needy, to help the less privileged, to love one another and be their brother's keeper. May be from my book, people can see things in a different way and find out that there is so much happiness in this world. The little things that we ignore, that we don't care about, are the greatest things that will bring us joy and happiness and our worries will be no more.

# CHAPTER 3

# MY INSPIRATION

I then began to think loudly again, what is it that inspires me? What is it that makes me happy? I knew it right away, it was my children. They mean the world to me. Seeing them grow up is a life changer for me. When I am in a bad mood, my six years old son Jason will come and hug me and say mom I love you. When I'm cranky that my 3 month old Jordan is awake all night, he gives me a cute smile that melts my heart and I quickly forget about the sleepless nights. Those are the moments I cherish, a natural gift from heaven.

I believe that everyone has that thing that inspires them, that thing that brings out the best in you that makes you want to do your best in everything you do. It can be the daily kiss and hug from your spouse when they leave the house, or it can be the exciting welcome you get from your pet dog or cat when you come back from work, it can be a call from a friend to check up on you and to know how you are doing, it can be your neighbor that greets you when you come outside your house, it can be anything around you that brings you joy, anything natural.

I began to see that it's not TV or internet that controls my happiness, it's what I do with people around me which was the light that shines beside me. At this point, I was sure this was my calling. A calling to reach out to the needy, poor, hurting, less privileged, sick, orphans, oppressed, hungry and the emotionally distressed.

I began to smile at anyone I see, I greet people on my way, I offer to help people in need in my own little way and most of all, I decided to follow my passion which was to write inspirational books, a book that will touch lives, and make people live a better life with people around them, a book that will motivate people to extend their hands to the needy, the oppressed, the hungry, the sick, the poor and the emotionally distressed. Yes, this is my calling, this is what makes me happy, it's my passion and now it's my new job.

# CHAPTER 4

# INNER JOY

It's getting late, the weather has changed drastically, it's now cool, and Chicago weather is not always predictable. I think of what good things I should do for myself and for my kids today. An outing sounds like a good idea, probably to a restaurant. Jason likes Chinese buffets and so do I. We've not been to a restaurant in a long while; today seems like a good day for it.

The food was nice; it was just what I needed to make my day a little fun. We drove home, changed into our warm clothing and headed straight to the park. There were so many kids playing in the park, the ducks were swimming in the pond. Jason made friends right away with the kids in the park. Jordan was peacefully sleeping in his car seat. As I look at the kids playing, it reminded me of my childhood, how free we were then. We played with sands, built castles with wet clay. I could remember the silly things I did when I was a kid, when I and my sister tried our first cooking skills with empty tin cans and we made fire with dry tree branches like we were in camp. It made me happy to see that my kids are happy and free.

I began to see that my inner joy comes from being happy and free. Happiness cannot be bought, it's the little things we do that makes us happy and gives us inner joy. Being in a state of happiness reflects in our daily work. It makes us a better person because the reflection of happiness which gives us inner joy is transferred to others.

If we are happy, it changes the atmosphere around us. People can feel it and they warm up to you. The effect of happiness in our lives is magical to our surrounding. Anytime I'm happy, I'm moved, I sing, I get to do a lot of work at home and so it can be for you.

Whether it's at work, school, home, meeting, conference, business, or church, the reflection of happiness sends a powerful message to the people around you. It can move you to do the unexpected for others. It can make you think of good things, stay positive and be helpful to your community. I have found happiness by looking at the little things we ignore, and I can say that my perception to life is so much better.

It's beginning to get cold, so it's time for us to go. Jason was sad to leave the park, but it's not over yet, we are going to be coming back more frequently. It's the start of summer and there will be many more park plays. I went home feeling good, feeling a sense of achievement, feeling energized. Even though there was no TV and internet, I felt so peaceful and relaxed. It was a fulfilling day.

# CHAPTER 5

# CARING FOR OTHERS

The sound of the rain and thunder woke me up. I looked at my time, it was 5 am. I can't believe how much I slept; I must have slept off early, because the lights were on. What a way to start the day on a Wednesday. I went to check the kids, they were sound asleep, and they were exhausted too. A glass of water and a fresh fruit is what I need now. I grab an apple from the fridge, and I picked up a magazine to read. It was Oprah magazine. Oprah is one woman I admire so much, she has a big heart, and is also a woman of substance, she inspires me and I love to read her magazine.

The thunder and lightning outside became intense, my kids wake up, I can hear the sound of the train speeding, and the sound of the early morning birds chirping outside. Then suddenly, it was quiet, the noise outside disappeared. This was a time of meditation, a time to think about how I will spend my day today. But first of all, I need to pray. Early Morning Prayer and meditation is a routine I'm used to since childhood.

I began to make my list of to do's. Today was supposed to be the court case with the banks concerning my mortgage, but it was shifted to next month. I still have a chance to get an income before next month; maybe the banks will then work with me. I was energized, I picked up my script and I continue to write.

Later that day, I thought about people I need to call. Is there anyone of my friends that needs encouragement? What about my cousins and family? A call to check up on them is what I felt like doing at that moment. You can never tell the joy you derive from checking up on others, it can be a friend, family or anybody you know that is lonely, or worried, or going through any type of difficulties. Maybe a call can brighten their day and it makes a whole lot of difference in their lives for the rest of the day.

I picked up the phone, and I called my sister, after that I called my brother and then my parents, they were all doing fine. Finally I called my Uncle, he was fine as well. Coming from a family of ten, I can't call everybody at once, so I share the days I check up on all of them, at least once a week. It made me feel happy, it brought a sense of belonging and knowing that you are not alone in this world, that there are people out there that you care for and really care about you as well.

Sometimes, the activities of our day are so overwhelming that we tend to forget to call our loved ones, the people we care about and the people that care about us. I got a call that changed my life, a call that made me find my passion in the lowest moments of my life, which was to write Inspirational Books. You can be that person for someonelse.

# CHAPTER 6

# THE ULTIMATE FAITH

The day went by so fast; we still have cupcakes and cookies to make and a visit to the library to use the internet. Today, I want to make a nice lunch treat for my kids. Spaghetti and meatballs is Jason's favorite. The aroma of my cooking excited Jason, it smells so good mom, "he said". We enjoyed our lunch and set out to the library.

Jason borrowed a lot of books. He just wants to read and read. It's amazing how Jason gets so interested in reading a lot of books. The books I read to him as a baby worked for him. I'm doing the same thing with Jordan as well; hopefully both of them will be great authors and writers someday. My mailbox had a lot of mails, some were from job recruiters. I quickly replied their emails, who knew that such messages will come in my email when my home internet was off.

When I got home, I was so exhausted. I tried to take a nap, suddenly I was woken up by the ring on my phone, and it was from a job employer. I had my first phone interview for a contract job as a Benefit Advisor position with my former employer. I looked at my time; it was 2:30pm. Who knew that such a call would come in. I've been endlessly applying for a job with no interview set. It just occurred to me that when the right time comes, you won't have to struggle for it. If something is meant for you, you won't need to suffer so much for it; it comes naturally with a little effort. At that time, you feel that all hope is lost, and you are waiting for the worst to happen, that's when miracles happen.

I just had my first interview for almost a year I've been applying for a job and it came when I almost lost hope of searching for a job, when my internet and TV was off, when I've found happiness and joy with the people and things around me, when I have found my calling and created a job for myself. A job that cost me nothing but a notebook and a pen; a job that will motivate people to change lives through my inspirational books. I knew that something great is about to start in my life. A job interview; a job offer hopefully; an income is on my way, that will help me live a good life and fulfill my dreams.

When I was growing up, I remember my prayers, I always say, "Lord, bless me abundantly, so I can live a good live and most importantly; to help the poor and the needy". Everything is coming back together now. There is power in the word of mouth. My long lost prayers is manifesting and becoming a reality. It can be the same for you, whatever you ask the Lord in prayers, even if you don't get it at the moment, don't be discouraged, he has a perfect time to answer your prayers, but be rest assured that he hears you and will give you the best of what you ask in his own time; a time you will be ready to receive it. If only we can see the future, we will have fewer worries, but believing and having faith in God will carry us through from our stormy paths to the paths of success, happiness, peace and prosperity.

# CHAPTER 7

# LOVE IN SHARING

Another day is here, the noise of the plowing machine out-side was so loud. The workers were cutting the flowers and mowing the lawn. I can smell fresh cut flowers; I can't believe its Friday already. The weather is just right, the sun is shining and the wind is blowing. What a perfect day for a car wash, before I forget, I need to call my provider to fix my internet and TV again.

The week went by so fast. As I'm waiting for a response back from my past job interviews, I have to use this weekend to hopefully get something tangible out of my job applications. I know that as long as you work hard towards something, with-out giving up, you will get what you desire. Believe me, it is depressing to be unemployed for a very long time with no income coming in, it is not healthy and can result to other physical and emotional distress, but when you think about it this way;"If God can feed the birds of the air and shelter them, what more a human being who is made in the likeness of him". This is my favorite quotation from the Holy Bible. For a moment, I stop thinking about my financial situation and I just give everything I do my best shot and leave the rest to God. Whatever will be, will be.

Later in the day, I went online and it was a miraculous moment, a job offer, an employment agreement letter from the past interview as a Benefit Advisor, I thought for a minute, that it's not real. What can be better than seeing such a letter? I knew that there is a reason for everything, It's almost 2 yrs of being unemployed, I had my second child and then the job comes. So now, everything is beginning to make meaning, if only we can have patience and watch his miracles manifest, if only we know what God has in stock for us, if only we can see the future, we would worry less.

I felt I need to give back to show appreciation. I only had $5 in my bag, so I went out and I found a charity box and dropped it. There is love in sharing, I might not have any cash left in my hands, but my joy is enough for me. When I donate, it makes me feel happy that I'm helping people in need. You can't imagine how much happiness you derive from giving. You are always a blessing to someone, especially when you give.

# CHAPTER 8

# MY JOURNEY STARTS

The past month has been so hectic. It's the first day of August. How time flew so fast. Summer is almost over and school will resume soon. I started work already, and did not forget my writing job, it was my passion. Anytime I'm not at work, I work on my inspirational book. My writing job brought out that hidden passion that I never realized that I could have.

I also started writing articles for clients on an article writing site. I even rewrote an article on a movie. Even though the writing skills paid a few dollars for each article, it trained me on how to write a good article through extensive online research and tireless readings in the internet and library, I was getting better with my writing skills. My office job lasted for 8 months and I went into unemployment again during the following winter. I was not sad at my time of struggle, for I knew that a greater job is ahead of me.

I received all the benefits that I could get from my employer and by summer, I started training on certification courses for my dream job. As I was doing this, my house foreclosed. I was not afraid for one day, because I knew that there is a light shining beside me through the people around me. That is why I am here today, homeless in my own home, enrolling on lucrative job trainings, knowing that the purpose of all these is one thing, "to fulfill my dreams, to reach out to the poor, the needy, helpless, hungry, disadvantaged women and children, and being an inspiration to my own children.

In a few months, I was forced to leave my home due to foreclosure, and I moved into a hotel and stayed there for about 5 months. Things were so rough and hard for me, every day I prayed, I say to God' "Give me just this day, my daily bread" and tomorrow will take care of itself. And my God showed himself to me, many times that period through my wonderful family and friends, especially my Mom, Dad, Kelly, Obi, Uzoma, Ramona Chris, Charito, Rita and Ugonna whom I call my shinning angels. They are wonderful and I love them.

Within a few months, I got an international job appointment from my home country Nigeria, to work at the University of Nigeria technology center. My hard work, job training, graduate studies and years of experiences were not in vain any more. I remembered that I have been destined for something great. I look forward to fulfilling my dreams now, starting from my home country, where I grew up, at the University of Nigeria.

I look forward to contribute, and to be a part of a great change in the African community, especially being a part of that voice; that source of inspiration for women and children in Africa; in my home country Nigeria; and the United States who gave me a citizenship, accommodated me, trained me and most of all, taught me how to contribute to my society. I look forward to a bright future.

I did not know that writing was my passion and will be an avenue for me to fulfilling my dreams in serving others, but I found out that all my sufferings, worries, fears, disappointments and pain was my preparation for greater things to come in the future and I can't wait to embrace it. Believe, have faith, be patient, persevere, have passion are all what I hear in my mind when I meditate, hearing God's word over and over in my head saying "Fear not, for I am with you"

Now my journey has just begun and more inspirational books will be coming your way, relax and enjoy your reading.

CPSIA information can be obtained at www.ICGtesting.com
Printed in the USA
BVOW08s0420090813

328062BV00002B/258/P